ORIGINS AND EARLY TRADITIONS OF STORYTELLING

ORIGINS AND EARLY TRADITIONS OF STORYTELLING

John Harrell

York House, Kensington, California

First Edition

York House, Publishers
148 York Avenue
Kensington, California 94708

Library of Congress Catalog Card Number: 82-51285

Greek caricature of Aesop and Fox

INTRODUCTION

For many reasons you and I today are storytellers. A school teacher discovers that history or geography comes alive for students when a regional tale is told. A psychiatrist is pleased with a patient's progress after they have explored the depths of a myth together. A community center leader finds that a street gang responds to a story of unexpected tenderness in a cruel world. Or one might become involved in story telling because it sounds like a good way to cope with our times of radical change, or because it is the current thing to do.

However we came to this important juncture in our lives, we are storytellers. And if we have not already wondered about and explored the origins and traditions of our vocation, then the time is now. Having immersed ourselves in dozens of story books and having started to tell tales, we automatically sense the need to be aware of our roots in this ancient art. Our inclination is right, for such awareness gives depth to our tellings and supports us when we have a feeling of being out on a limb all alone. Such knowledge guides us in our growth as storytellers and helps to curb us from going into dead ends. It opens unthought-of possibilities and challenges us with goals and ideals worth striving for.

This essay is both a culmination of long, thoughtful study and an outcome from a workshop I led as part of a week's conference on storytelling held at Danville, California, in the summer of 1982. It conveys not only the material I came prepared to share, but also the questions and perplexities of the workshop participants as the week went along. Honing of basic questions goes on in such a workshop and often, surprisingly, answers come like penetrating darts that startle one into new awareness. I hope that somehow I can share that experience with you, as well as pass along basic facts about storytelling and my interpretation.

Having said that much about the origins of this essay, I ought to add a bit more. In the spirit of the aoidos, I determined a year ahead of the Danville engagement to lecture for the week without notes or written outline, simply having a framework in mind and calling up from memory what was important for us as storytellers. In the same informal way immediately after, I wrote this summary free of notes or reference books, except for spot checks, and relying on the storyteller's tools of memory and clearness of inner vision of how things happened, once upon a time.

Surprisingly, almost all the information in this essay is fairly recent. Whether the question is Linear B, or Gilgamesh tablets, or the earliest *Homo erectus*, or Mycenae, the findings are only decades old if that much, at most within our century, and all currently debated in scholarly circles. That has been one of the intriguing parts of doing the research, for while the search is into the distant past, the clues are only coming to light in our lifetime. In this influx of new data, upturning old scientific and academic tenets, cross-disciplines are emerging and new ones being established.

The attempt here is informally to set a framework for further research and combining of disciplines to clarify our special field of interest. Some of the areas have to do with development of the brain and psychology in general, the development of the organs of speech, the invention of language, the startling moment when man became artist, societal development, the origins of religion, myth, and legends and their diffusion, the overwhelming consequences of passing from illiterate to literate beings, the effects of naive tellers and the roles of professionals in the shaping of storytelling. These are some of the critical questions and the wonders we can explore for our better telling.

At the close of each section ahead you will find a bibliography. The titles are not the bases of the sections — hundreds of books, articles, conversations, and correspondences lie behind these few pages. The listings are suggestions for your further reading or listening if you want to explore on your own. You will find a line in these titles, and below the line will be some technical books too important to omit while too specialized to recommend casually. If you have the zest for it, plow on!

I want wholeheartedly to acknowledge my indebtedness and express my appreciation to the Very Reverend Sherman E. Johnson, biblical scholar and archeologist, and Professor William Anderson of the Department of Classics, University of California at Berkeley, who have read this manuscript and have generously offered their criticisms and advice. Of course, I take full responsibility for any errors in fact and all interpretations of data in what I have written.

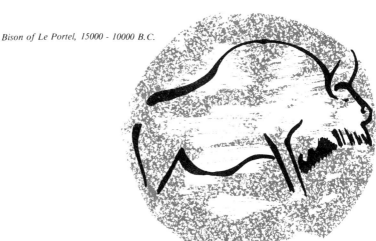

Bison of Le Portel, 15000 - 10000 B.C.

I

THE GREAT RIFT VALLEY

The wonder that is man has beginnings that are reached only by reversing time unthinkable millions of years and retracing shadowy steps to a parched stretch along the eastern coast of Africa. There in the Great Rift Valley our story begins with ancestors we can hardly recognize as our progenitors. Below their growing neocortex lay a primitive brain, made up of the limbic system and the R-complex (R for Reptilian), millions of years still older, and passed on to us today. It is this old brain that accounts for some of our automatic responses to situations such as heights that parallel the experiences of our earliest ancestors who knew the perils as well as the safety of being tree dwellers. So to that extent our ancestry is responsible for the effectiveness of one of storytelling's basic ingredients, for the suspense of plot bears close resemblence to suspension from tree limbs, and making daring advances in that way through forest is like living through the accumulating events that create a story. The possibility that we, as storytellers, may be engaged in an activity that arouses responses so primeval must cause us to wonder at the art we possess.

During the millions of years of continuing adaptations to changing food supplies and ways of life, the strand that would lead to *Homo sapiens sapiens* evolved, still largely in Africa. Then with the close of the last ice age, the glaciers that had covered much of the northern hemisphere began to retreat, making vast regions habitable to our ever more mobile and intelligent forebears. With much of earth's water still locked in glacial masses, sea levels were lower than today and there probably was a land bridge linking Tunisia, Siciliy, and Italy, opening the way from Africa into the continent of Europe. Rounding the end of the Mediterranean, the Levant spread eastward, making possible a dispersion into the continent of Asia. Along these two natural pathways, into Europe and Asia our forebears moved. So difficult is it for us to comprehend the time span involved in the dispersion of early man that we are tempted to regard these movements as migrations. For the in-

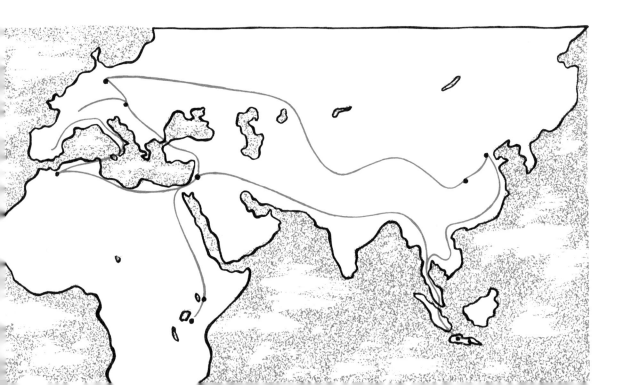

dividuals involved, however, there could have been no awareness whatsoever of the expansion, so slowly it occurred. To help gain a sense of the elapse, consider that during this period of moving from tropics into colder climates, skin pigmentation was changing and growing lighter, body hair was modifying to make possible changes in sweat glands and skin pores. Depending on the direction of their slow progression into differing environments, unique characteristics were developing which we can now recognize as the beginnings of racial differentiations. Thus, while Java and Heidelberg man were markedly different, they both were *Homo erectus*, only they had adapted to differing conditions and ways of life.

As storytellers, our chief inheritance from *Homo erectus* is the pit fire. The myth of Prometheus has events exactly right, for Prometheus' gift of fire to the first man made him like the gods and set him apart from all other living creatures. With fire, *Homo erectus* began to cook meat which made it more tender, and as a consequence his teeth and jaw underwent modifications — teeth becoming smaller, the jaw narrower, the pharynx lengthier, and the root of the tongue deeper — leading to the vocal apparatus that permits the greatly varied articulation of sounds required by human speech which is the storyteller's medium. Fire also gave *Homo erectus* warmth, and at night it kept preying animals at a distance. As terrifying as wild fire can be, controlled in a pit or banked by stones it gives security and comfort. And, too, by its light it lengthened waking hours, giving space for recreation. The storyteller today who gathers a group around a campfire or who lights a candle for story hour at a library is recapitulating a custom of cameraderie that stems from such prehistoric times and has continued unbroken to this day.

In this continued custom of gathering around the pit fire, by the time of the emergence of *Homo sapiens* dance as a communal expression developed. Certainly dance is oldest of the arts, but it must have soon been followed by percussion accompaniment — clapping of hands, slapping of palms on thighs, stomping with feet, eventually the tapping of sticks. We can suppose that the developing vocal mechanism was employed, too, with repetitions and patterns of sounds with variations of pitch. So the pit fire ritual-like custom elaborated itself over millennia.

One of the strangest interludes in the development of *Homo sapiens* was Neanderthal man. His brain was as large as ours today and in a smaller body. Because of this ratio it is possible he was more intelligent than we, although the shape of his skull, sweeping sharply back from a prominent brow ridge, suggests limitations. But further, the mechanism for speech had greatly developed in Neanderthal, so with his advanced intellect he was fully capable of a developed language, and it is certain that he made this giant step. Certain, because every biological creature has always made the best of its potential to assure its survival. As to his character there is reason to believe he was of a pacific disposition, and within his extended family or clan there was a bond of respect and love that is discernible in his burial customs. The fact he practiced burial to prevent the dead from desecration by scavenger beasts gives strong evidence of his sense of the individual's integrity. Too, precious objects accompanied the corpse at burial, and in one instance meat was offered for the after-life of the deceased. And the most touching token of Neanderthal's sense of bond and love for the departed is an instance where he covered the body with flowers before enclosing it in the earth.

From this scant information, we can conclude that a belief regarding death had already begun and that Neanderthal's sentiments about persons and his sense of an after-life were communicated by word of mouth and ritual over tens of thousands of years. He perceived life as more than mundane, that a realm of the spirit surrounds us, and that our existence is framed in eternity. These conclusions are incontrovertible.

To return to the continued custom of the pit fire, Neanderthal is certain to have made his contributions, and exceedingly important ones. At quiet times around the fire he began informal storytelling, a tradition that continues to this day among naive tellers. The subject might have been the sort common among all hunters and fishers, or out of his family/clan life the hilarious recollections of gaffs, tomfoolery, tricks, or more seriously, "just so" stories of how things came to be. Of equal or greater importance, in the ceremonial dance he substituted words for the singing of nonsense sounds. And because lyrics carry meaning and subject matter, nobler thoughts of consequence, perhaps embodying his mythology of life and death, gave intent to the lyrics he composed for the dance. And so the roots of epic poetry came into being. Such is our indebtedness to Neanderthal man.*

The time span of *Homo neanderthalensis* was approximately from 100,000 years ago to 40,000, and then mysteriously that extraordinary creature, who lived on earth for sixty millennia, disappeared without leaving living descendants. His legacy, however, became the inheritance of another line of *Homo sapiens,* Cro-Magnon man, who appeared just before Neanderthal withdrew and in a remarkably short period of 30,000 years formed the bridge to modern man. Incredibly, during a stretch of this time he reached a peak of creativity and excellence perhaps comparable only to the birth of civilization in Sumer, the golden age of Greece, and the Renaissance of Europe.

Our image of Cro-Magnon must undergo radical change if our impressions of him stem from films and comic books or even the anthropological guesses of only a generation or so ago. Like Neanderthal, Cro-Magnon possessed a brain as large as ours, but unlike Neanderthal there was no brow ridge and the cranium was truly modern in form,

---

*I do not suggest the theories of J. G. Frazer, Jane Harrison, and Gilbert Murray, or Mircea Eliade, that the world's myths have devolved from rituals. The pit fire is only an instance of a perpetuated, elemetary custom that from the beginning lent itself to becoming an informal ritual of bondedness among family or clan, a time for passing from conscious responses about the urgencies of day to the unconscious dream work of sleep. In this communal setting and as part of the transition between our two modes of thought, storytelling finds its most natural milieu. In this instance, then, the custom or informal ritual of the fire pit is not so much the cause of myths and other stories as the occasion for them.

allowing for the full development of frontal lobes and their functions as we have them today. His physique, too, presented a modern appearance, and far from being a naked ape, he tanned hide and sewed clothing which he elaborated with decorations. Grandly he wore arm bands, anklets and necklaces. And his tool kit radically expanded over the kit he inherited.

It is from his diversified tool kit that we gain the first hint of his bravado in excellence. Beyond the scrapers needed for preparing hides and the needles to sew them into clothing, for instance, there appear what anthropologists call "laurel leaves." These fragile objects chipped from flint offer no possible practical use. They could have been made for no other purpose than for the sheer delight in the skill of the maker and for the aesthetics of the final product. Such evidence makes us aware that we have come into contact with the kind of mind that is the glory of man. One wonders what has been lost to us because the media worked in were more perishable than stone, but already we are prepared to be astounded by Cro-Magnon.

But first, we must comprehend his geographic daring and expansion over the earth during his existence.

Anthropologists are still puzzled as to where Cro-Magnon originated and by the paths of his advance. The greatest concentration of fossils is in France and Spain where Cro-Magnon reached his heights, but the oldest fossil yet found comes from Israel. A map of his distribution throughout the world, however, shows us clearly how he spread out from the territories of Neanderthal until he inhabited every continent on earth, including Australia which was cut off from Southeast Asia by the fathoms of the Java trench, and how he got there is a quandry. With this geographic expansion and burgeoning population, we must suppose that the earliest myths and rituals, whose origins were among Neanderthal, were also carried along while at the same time undergoing change and refinement, and also added to by new stories and rites that reflected a growing insight into the nature of life and the world. The nightly gathering at a pit fire, a custom reaching back to *Homo erectus*, would guarantee a great deal of continuity in the dance, the music, the songs and myths even over such a long stretch of time. The naively told tales of lesser import, separated from the constancy factors of rhythm and music, would be far more open to change and novelty.

Exactly how Cro-Magnon's stories went or what they were about we can never know directly, but there are some clues from which we can make deductions. One such clue is what anthropologists call the baton de commandement. This common object was carved from an antler with a hole drilled through one end. Most often the baton was given elaboration by incised patterns or depictions of animals. But what are we to make of this curious object that has no apparent use? The one thing clear is that a thong could pass through the hole and the object be carried tied about the waist, for instance. The first guess of anthropologists was that it was a symbol of authority and so it was dubbed baton de commandement and the designation has stuck. Now, many of the frequent herringbone or other decorations on the baton correspond with similar decorations on a few other carry-along objects made by Cro-Magnon. Microscopic examinations of the "designs" prove that in fact they are notations. Not a thought-out whole, as a design is,

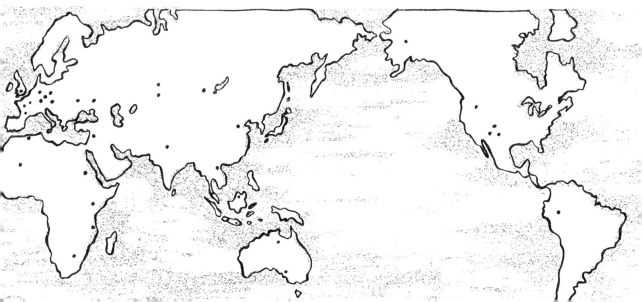

but an accumulation of marks made over a period of time. The proof of this observation is that the incisions were cut with different markers and not as a craftsman would create a repetitive design with a single tool at one sitting. It was Alexander Marshack who proposed further that the notations recorded the recurring phases of the moon and that Cro-Magnon had invented a lunar calendar. Marshack's conclusion is widely accepted today, although not universally. If he is correct, then we know that Cro-Magnon had a keen sense of the rhythms of celestial phenomena and developed from them a guide to times of year on earth. But since Cro-Magnon was not a planter, but a hunter-gatherer, such calendric calculation was unnecessary. The answer to our natural query may be that after Cro-Magnon's wanderings in pursuit of game and sources of vegetable foods, he had a calendar to alert him when it was time to return to a traditional site where the larger tribe, to which his clan belonged, would assemble for periodic rites.*

The caves at Altamira and Lascaux in Spain and France would be two such traditional gathering places, and there were hundreds more. Anthropologists who have written about the caves invariably report that there is a sense of holy sanctuary about them, a sense that is

*Possibly we are unknowing heirs of the baton de commandement. In the Bodleian Library of Oxford University there is a collection of clog almanacs or runic calendars, remnants of a tradition that entered England with the Danish kings. These almanacs are in the shape of a four-sided stick with a handle at one end around which a thong was tied and the almanac hung by a fireplace. Along each edge of the stick are notches representing days and weeks of a quarter year, and extending from the notches are runic characters representing the feast days of the Christian calendar. Could there be a connection with Cro-Magnon's baton with its calendric notches? I was discussing the notion with a visiting Swiss theologian whose face suddenly lit up with the excitement of discovery. In Switzerland, a lector who reads the appointed lessons of the Christian calendar at service is inexplicably called "the wooden stick." Could it be that the Swiss lector, known as "the wooden stick," has his title from the runic calendar of the Norse, and in turn, from Cro-Magnon's baton? At least it is fun to consider a possible connection among these three events.

heightened by the magnificence and great age of the paintings by Cro-Magnon that still cover the walls and ceilings of the deepest recesses. Access to these vaulted spaces, hundreds of yards from their entrance, is by way of narrow passages, the clearance overhead sometimes dropping so that one must crawl, or there are pools through which one must wade up to arm pit. So Cro-Magnon, carrying a rock hollowed out to contain animal fat and with a wick of fibers making a lamp, went in solemn procession to his holy place of meeting, a tradition perhaps begun by Neanderthal.

We can surmise the ritual that was enacted or the myths that were told had in part to do with the seasons and passing of time, perhaps a recollection, preserved in story, of the last ice age. But the paintings of the caves give us further hints. The first and primary observation about the paintings is their overwhelming magnificence. They equal in grandeur, in perception of nature and artistic expression, the heights of achievement at any time. They go so far beyond functional representations needed for "sympathetic magic" that it is witless to suggest that that was their purpose. Two facts mitigate against such an explanation. One, of all the animals portrayed, only 15% indicate ritual wounds. The other, two preliminary drawings have been found in caves from which enlargements were made on the walls nearby, all of which suggests a grander motivation than simply drawing a schematic form for the purpose of magic. The motivation, of course, was to create art! To create a visual presentation that expressed the wonder Cro-Magnon experienced in his relationship with the world of mammoths, bulls, and reindeer. And he powerfully succeeded as the result of great labor, for years of experience in drawing lie behind the deft, single stroke that outlines with incredible spirit and realism the course of a bull's neck and back. And, too, consider the joint labor of bringing timbers and erecting a scaffold for the artist, and the necessary grinding of pigments, the making of brushes, the holding of lamps. An entire community supported the artist's hand that drew the brush across the cave surface.

"The Sorcerer" of Les Trois Frères. After H. Breuil

So we are led to believe that the mythology created and relayed had also to do with nature and respect of animal life as well as an interest in its fecundity and supply as food. It is my conviction that a race that achieved such heights cast its myths in sung poetry of equal beauty and incomparable spirit. What follows is a model to test what might have been sung, putting our clues all together and adding the possibility that in the recitation there was communal participation. Perhaps we even know how the singer of the myth appeared, for here is one of the few representations of a human being among all the depictions of animals created by Cro-Magnon. Curiously, when he turned his eye on his own kind his artistic capacity left him, but we are still grateful for the data he supplied.

I

In the long ago, earth was always green.
There was no dread, white winter as we know.
Forever earth was rich with the green of grasses
And the green of shrubs, of vines and trees,
Each bearing the goodness of fruits and nuts.

   Antelope had food to eat and more.
   Bear had food to eat and more.

Boar and bison had plenty.
There was plenty for everyone,
For man and every other creature.

> *Life Dance I* (women's chorus)
> Every creature had enough and more.
> Every creature had its fill.
> Their bellies swelled. They swelled with life.
> They dropped their young in return to earth.

Every day Sun-god rose on green earth.
Sun-god gave light and warmth to earth.
And everyone was glad in Sun-god, except for Chaos-dragon.

II

Chaos-dragon had always lived in darkness.
Darkness always hid Chaos and no one
Knew that dragon was living in the darkness.
Then Chaos-dragon came out. He left the darkness.
He flew up into the sky. He bellowed.
He breathed at Sun-god to put him out.
He breathed again and again at Sun-god,
But Sun-god would not be put out.
Chaos-dragon opened his jaws. Wide open
Chaos-dragon open his jaws and swallowed Sun-god.

There was no light. There was only darkness.
There was no warmth. There was only cold.
There was no green on earth. There was only ice and snow.

> Antelope could not graze. Bear went hungry.
> Boar and bison went hungry.
> The she-beasts did not drop their young.
> They stood in the ice and snow. They froze.

> *Hunting Party I* (men's chorus)
> Where are the fleet footed antelope?
> Where are the bear and bison?

17

Give us a chance at them and we'll bring
Food for all and thank them for it.

But there was nothing for anyone to eat.
There was nothing for the hunting party to hunt.

III

Sun-god grew angry that Chaos-dragon had swallowed him.
Sun-god would not be swallowed and be gone forever.
Sun-god burned through Chaos-dragon.
From inside dragon, Sun-god burned through.
Chaos-dragon hurt. He was seared. He bellowed.
Just so, Sun-god came out of him.
Sun-god was in the sky again, and Chaos-dragon crept back into darkness.

Ice and snow melted. Cold became warm.
Earth was green again. Green covered the earth.

Antelope had food to eat again and more.
Bear had food to eat again and more.
Boar and bison had plenty.
There was plenty for everyone.

Life Dance II (women's chorus)
Every creature has enough and more.
Every creature has its fill.
Our bellies swell. They swell with life.
They drop their young in return to earth.

The she-beasts began to drop their young again.
There was plenty for the hunting party to hunt.
Everyone was glad in Sun-god again.

Hunting Party II (men's chorus)
Now there are the fleet-footed antelope.
Now the bear and bison.
Give us the heart to take their lives;

They will give us food for the time
And we will thank them for it.

IV

Ever since and every year Chaos-dragon comes from his darkness,
The place where he lives that no one can see.
Chaos-dragon flies into the sky and tries to swallow Sun-god.
Chaos-dragon opens his jaws at Sun-god. His jaws begin to close.
Sun-god will not let himself be swallowed ever again.
He comes back out of dragon's mouth before he is swallowed.
Sun-god always comes back out and Chaos-dragon returns to his place.
Sun-god always has the better of Chaos-dragon.

Sun-god is the dawning and the evening of our lives.
Sun-god is the begining of our next day.

Like the other fires that have burned brightly for a short time on occasion during human history, the brilliance of Altamira, Lascaux and other contemporary achievements of Cro-Magnon was soon followed by retrogression. The high, noble purpose, the spiritual exaltation, and the dazzle of intellectual discovery waned, and while cave painting continued, it fell into vacuous pedestrianism without a hint of creative elan. Just so, about 10,000 years ago Cro-Magnon passed quietly and uneventfully into modern man, but bequeathing him a great legacy from his past, not the least, his stories and myths.

The First Men. Time-Life Books, N.Y., 1973
Tom Prideaux, *Cro-Magnon Man.* Time-Life Books, N.Y., 1973
Carl Sagan, *The Dragons of Eden.* Random House, N.Y., 1977

Bjorn Kurton, *Dance of the Tiger: A Novel of the Ice Age.* Pantheon Books, N.Y., 1980

G. S. Kirk, *The Nature of Greek Myths.* Penguin Books, N.Y., 1974

Alexander Marshack, *The Roots of Civilization.* McGraw-Hill Book Co., N.Y., 1972

Gilgamesh and Enkidu with the Bull of Heaven

II

SUMER

The dawn of civilization both recorded the past and directed the future course of storytelling. In fact, the invention of writing created a tension between oral tradition and fixed texts that consumes us to this day. So this phase, a scant 6,000 years after Cro-Magnon, is critical in the development of storytelling.

After our global view of Cro-Magnon we must now narrow our range of vision to "the land of two rivers," to the area of the Tigris and Euphrates. When we understand the geography of this place we will have a major clue to the birth of civilization. From a high plateau in the north, the land drops to a flat plain, and coursing down the fall in elevation two great rivers wash through the arid land below, joining as they enter the Persian Gulf. (The Gulf today is silted at the mouth of the rivers so that the coast is farther south.) To the east are the Zagros Mountains which effectively cut off the neighboring land so that beyond the range, as years go by, there will be a cultural lag of centuries. By the same token, however, as Asiatic influences penetrated the eastern region little was felt west of the Zagros. From the rivers, to the west were the north Arabian steppes, completing the boundaries of Mesopotamia.

In the descent of the Tigris and Euphrates, the rivers washed down silt, and overflowing their banks periodically, deposited it in the plain and marshes, leaving an extraordinarily rich soil for later agriculture. Except for palm, the area was treeless, even on the higher plateau, and the land was devoid of rock for future building material. The barenness was amplified by intense heat from the sun that rarified the atmosphere, making the area all the more inhospitable to man. And here, once again, we are greatly aggravated by our lack of information, but from somewhere a non-Semitic people, the Sumerians, entered the land of two rivers and settled there, displacing the few original inhabitants. They brought with them knowledge of agriculture and began to exploit the fertile soil, and they began to form independent settlements along the rivers which grew into sizable communities, each with its distinct autonomy and sense of loyalty to itself and its chief. There was nothing extraordinary about that, for with increasing populations everywhere the same pattern was developing. Periodically, however, the great rivers, swelled from torrential rainfall in the north, overflowed their

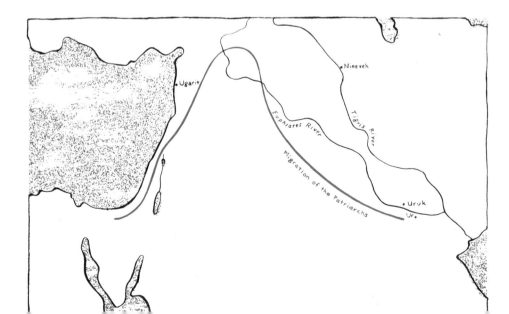

banks exceedingly and brought devastation throughout the lower plain, often with total loss of life in broad areas. If the Sumerians were to remain in this land, it was necessary to bring the two rivers under control. As a result, for the first time in human development, a sizable population of separate units merged into a political body for the purpose of their mutual well being. With this move, Ur became the principal city and the center of the Sumerians. From this administrative center, plans were made for channeling the rivers with dikes and constructing a network of canals that fairly and safely distributed water to local farmers throughout the entire region. Such a massive undertaking required organization, a hierarchy of authority, and a means of accounting for individual labor by the levee workers, assessments and collections from farmers. Out of this came the invention of writing which is the watershed between prehistory and history. The period was mid-fourth millennium.

The first thing to remark about the invention of writing is its medium, which was the ever-abundant clay that was available at hand. The clay would be shaped into small flat bricks or tablets and incised with a wedge-shaped stick. The first efforts, which merely concerned themselves with registering concrete objects and quantities, were pictographic, but even so, because of the stylus, there was a degree of abstraction that soon led to symbolic forms. As the pictographs expanded in number, encompassing more and more words, the markings began to shift from being pictographs to being phonic symbols. With that shift, the written characters were used to represent any and all words in the spoken language. Because cuneiform is a phonetic system and not an alphabet, hundreds of characters and elaborate rules were required in order to embrace the entire spoken language. Scribal schools were established for the years of training eventually needed to become a professional scribe. But cuneiform was so successful that in the course of time it was used by many peoples, Semitic and non-Semitic, and in fact it endured longer than any system of writing since. And how fortunate for us that the medium was clay, for when it was

Development of cuneiform star representing heaven or god

23

baked it left us an imperishable record of those thousands of years.

At first, cuneiform was used only for the dreary work of tax accountants and the administrative details of the Tigris-Euphrates water control project and the like. But in an astonishing few hundred years we find it recording hymns of the mid-third millennium, and very soon thereafter poems of true majesty, such as the *Epic of Emmerkar,* from which comes this passage about a golden age before the "confusion of tongues" (Genesis 11:1).

In those days there was no snake, there was no scorpion, there was no hyena,
There was no lion, there was no wild dog, no wolf,
There was no fear, no terror,
Man had no rival.

In those days the land Shubur (East), the place of plenty, of righteous decrees,
Harmony-tongued Sumer (South), the great land of the "decrees of
   princeship,"
Uri (North), the land having all that is needful,
The land Martu (West), resting in security,
The whole universe, the people in unison,
To Enlil in one tongue gave praise.*

Because works such as this come to us in various versions, we know that they were not the product of single poets writing in the new medium, in the third millennium, but rather reflect the hymns and epics of a tradition reaching far back in time before the invention of writing. It is these first poetic writings that suggested the style of our model of prehistoric myth above. If the epic poetry of Cro-Magnon was cast differently, at least it was pointed in this direction.

Tragically, the first civilization, created by the Sumerians, was soon engulfed by the invasion of a Semitic warrior people, the Akkadians, who nonetheless had the good sense to adopt what they were unable to create on their own. So while the Akkadians behaved typically like conquerors, they respected the cultural values of the Sumerians and

*From *Sumerian Mythology* by Samuel Noah Kramer.

perpetuated them. For a time the Sumerians regained control of their land, only to be swept over by the Babylonians and they, in turn, by the Assyrians. By great good fortune, the Assyrian monarch, Ashur-banipal, decided to enhance his new palace at Nineveh with a library suitable for a king. Scribes in his library collected tens of thousands of cuneiform tablets, many in Akkadian and Sumerian, dating as much as 1,500 years earlier, making copies and translations, codifying and storing them in the palace library. Today that library has come to light and it is our principal means, along with archeological finds at Lagash and Nippur, of recovering the oldest story of mankind, the *Epic of Gilgamesh*. This epic happens also to be a magnificent work worthy to stand beside the poetry of any age, so let us pause and take a short look at it.

Gilgamesh was the young and lusty king of Uruk, strong and beautiful because he was two-thirds god and one-third man. While his people delighted in their king, he began to abuse his sovereignty and the people called on the god of Uruk, Anu, to make a man his equal to break his pride. So Enkidu was created from clay, the mirror image of Gilgamesh. A child of nature, he roamed the steppes, and ate and ran with the wild animals. Then the farmers and trappers complained that Enkidu was interfering in their lives, for he saved the wild animals from their traps. A temple harlot was sent to lie with Enkidu and so make him civilized and human. Then the wild animals fled from him, and he could no longer run with them, for his fleetness was gone.

When Enkidu heard that the king, Gilgamesh, lorded it over the people in the city, he went to confront him, and in a mighty wrestling match the two willful heroes came to a draw, and thereafter became fast companions. Together they accomplished a number of exploits that affronted the gods, including slaying the Bull of Heaven, and in recompense Enkidu was struck with illness and died. Gilgamesh lamented loudly the loss of his friend and anguished over the knowledge that his own life must also someday end. Not able to accept his mortality, Gilgamesh went in pursuit of eternal youth, passing through a mountain and crossing the waters of death. Then he spent time with the prototype of Noah and his wife whom only the gods had granted, after the flood, eternal life. In the end Gilgamesh returned to Uruk, broken of his hubris and content with his destiny, serving his people as a just and glorious king long to be remembered in his epic.

For thousands of years this story was retold, and more than any other subject, Gilgamesh was engraved on cylinder seals, the personal stamps used by ordinary citizens unable to write. In two broad migrations the poem has had effect on our inheritance, from the classical world of Greece and the biblical world of the Hebrews. For Homer's *Iliad* and *Odyssey* were doubtless influenced by the epic, and the flood story of *Genesis* was adapted directly from the Sumerian tradition. In minor details and major themes, again and again the epic records storytelling material, already ancient, that will surface anew in Greek mythology and Hebrew scriptures.

For once, we are not left in the dark about the transmission of story material, for we have written, historical evidence of how the *Epic of Gilgamesh* and other Mesopotamian myths and lore came into the possession of the Israelites. Where the two rivers empty into the Persian Gulf, on either side of the Sumerian capitol of Ur, lived two Semitic peoples, the Elamites and the Chaldeans. It was from "Ur of the Chaldees" that the first and great patriarch, Abraham, arose, driven by

Yahweh to father His people in a distant land. The path of the patriarchs' migration can be traced in the biblical record to the edge of Egypt, where Jacob and his sons and their families were given sanctuary by Joseph during the great famine. In turn, Moses and Aaron brought the Hebrews at last to the land promised by Yahweh to Abraham. During this migration, many stories from Ur were preserved, altered, and elaborated upon according to the unique insights of this religious people and recorded or referred to in the Old Testament repeatedly.

If we ask what storytelling was like during this period in Mesopotamia, we can assume that naive, amateur tellers continued to repeat informally the tales they knew from childhood and to invent new stories out of their lives or imagination. Telling was done for the sheer fun of it or for admonition of the young. The principal criterion would be the degree to which the teller successfully aroused the imagination of his hearers so that the stories took on reality, or triggered the unconscious mechanisms of humor, or reinforced the strictures and demands of the superego. Myths and epics, on the other hand, were recited by professional singers or priests. Many formal constraints hedged the telling and increased the criteria at the same time they provided the requisites for an art, for all art comes out of a discipline and results from having to deal with the problems it sets for itself. In that dealing, so critical to him, the artist comes to know himself and in the end it is his revelation of self which has also deeply contended with life that creates art.

For one thing, the epics and myths were still sung in performance. There had not yet come the degree of sophistication when lyrics detached themselves from music and became poetry in their own right, let alone become prose. We have a picture of a singer and her accompanist from the Standard of Ur (the designation, "Standard," is absolutely misleading but that is how it is known). This famous, complex work was a plaque decorating the sounding board of a musical instrument. It is made of fragile shell and lapis lazuli set in bitumen, and considering

the difficulty of the medium the result is admirable. Here is one small detail, greatly enlarged, from the complex whole showing a woman professional singer and her accompanist. If we examine the piece we notice a bull's head at the front of the lyre. This decorative device, like the scroll on the neck of instruments in our viol family today, was traditional, although there were a few alternatives. It is our guess that the tradition stems from the popularity of the Gilgamesh epic and the slaying of the Bull of Heaven. Several lyres, as pictured in the Standard of Ur, have survived and the gold and inlaid bull decorations are truly magnificent. If we want to hear what the instrument sounded like, there is the possibility. Anne Draffkorn Kilmer and her colleagues at the University of California built a replica of the Sumerian lyre in the British Museum and Dean Kilmer has recorded her decipherment of an Ugarit hymn, notated in cuneiform, dating about 1400 B.C. There are two disappointments in the recording. The text is not yet fully translatable, and we do not know, and never will know, the natural rhythm of the spoken words let alone the time values given the notes when sung. Still, the recording is an impressive experience.

One thing that strikes us as we contemplate the Standard of Ur is that there must be a mutually understood way for the story to be recited if these two professionals are going to keep their standing. There are going to be enough lapses of memory in spots anyway, requiring a bluffing through, but the whole performance cannot be one gigantic bluff, and besides, the audience knows well how the traditional material goes. Keen memory of how tradition gives the epic and skill in recreation at the moment of performance were absolutely necessary.

Lastly, we must deal with two related questions, knowing ahead of time that there is precious little to give answer, but sharpening the questions at least will give us a firmer grasp of serious problems. The first question is, Why did scribes, shortly after the invention of writing, begin to record the lyrics of sung epics and myths? Of course we are grateful they did because we have documentation of stories that were sung at the time and concrete evidence of the storytelling tradition in the antecedent period. But why the documentation at all, incomplete as it was without the music? Further, literacy was largely confined to the professional scribes, so for whom were the tablets intended? One motive that suggests itself is simply the scribal mind that enjoys collecting data and codifying them. Or was it the universally conservative nature of priesthoods that found enhanced power being in possession of a written record? However, the *Epic of Gilgamesh*, for instance, was not a sacred text but a secular work performed as entertainment. For the time being the question remains open.

The second question has to do with the consequences of a written record of storytelling. Once an oral tradition is written down it ceases to be the one thing and becomes another. To the romantic, it is like spilt milk, and reversing the process and recovering the former condition is an impossibility. It was this consequence that drove Milman Parry and Albert Lord in their monumental task of preserving on record the last of true oral epic storytellers in Europe before universal literacy and publication of transcriptions brought an end forever to the art. Once oral tradition becomes written two things happen. There is a permanent source for future storytellers to draw material from, and there is a rein on how much the storyteller can depart without, in effect, creating something new and wholly different. The book is closed, as it were, and if one is going to tell *that* story one must tell it *that* way. To tell it in

Gold bull's head on a lyre from Ur

29

another way is not to tell it at all, but to create something else. If a storyteller does not conclude *The Fairy* collected by Charles Perrault with "As for her sister, she made herself so odious that her own mother turned her out of the house, and the unhappy wretch having wandered about a good while without finding anybody to take her in, went to a corner of a wood and died," then he has not told Perrault's *The Fairy.*

The question we are dealing with here is so critical to storytelling, and to our self-understanding as storytellers, that we will have to return to it again, and all of us spend time sorting out our thoughts for a long time after.

John Gray, *Near Eastern Mythology.* Hamlyn House, N.Y., 1969

André Parrot, *Sumer: The Dawn of Art.* Golden Press, N.Y., 1961

N. K. Sandars, *The Epic of Gilgamesh.* Penguin Books, N.Y., 1972

Sounds from Silence: Recent Discoveries in Ancient Near Eastern Music (12" lp record with illustrated booklet). Bit Enki Publications, P.O. Box 9068, Berkeley, CA 94709

Samuel Noah Kramer, *Sumerian Mythology.* University of Pennsylvania Press, Philadelphia, 1972

Albert B. Lord, *The Singer of Tales.* Harvard University Press, Cambridge, 1960

James B. Pritchard, *Ancient Near Eastern Texts Relating to the Old Testament.* Princeton University Press, Princeton, 1955.

Gold Mycenaean burial mask

III

THE AEGEAN

The Cyclades in the Aegean Sea are worlds away from the land of two rivers. These very small islands, clustered off the coast of mainland Greece, were originally forested and the sea tempered the climate from extremes of heat and cold. The people who settled here brought with them their neolithic culture from the mainland. One telling example is a style of stone figurine, fiddle-shaped with a long neck and no head, still common about 3000 B.C. During the next thousand years, Cycladic figurines would evolve into new forms unique to their developing culture. And the people of the islands did lead the people of the mainland in cultural advancement. One reason might be that because of the size of the islands, they were forced to compress a growing population into towns of 1,000 and up to as many as 5,000 people. Food needs began to exceed the capacity of crop lands to produce, but the introduction of olives and grapes into the diet expanded the cultivable area as olive trees and grape vines would grow on hillsides that were not tillable. To make the system work, barter was necessary and specialization led to the beginning of trades and crafts among the city dwellers.

The next phase came easily, of exporting goods and importing grain and other basic needs. Companion to the burgeoning shipbuilding and maritime economy was piracy, and there was a good deal of that, too.

Apart from a few bookkeeping notations, however, this rising culture never stumbled onto writing, and we have only their figurines, their peculiar pottery and other artifacts, to tell us anything about their thoughts and feelings. We look and listen, but there is largely silence. They had, however, entered the Bronze Age as forerunners in the Aegean, and that was a landmark achievement.

South of the Cyclades is a major island, Crete. As early as 7000 B.C., long before the occupation of the Cyclades, settlers began arriving at Crete, probably from the Near East. After millennia, these settlers still simply existed on Crete and lagged behind their new neighbors on the tiny off-shore Cycladic islands, but with communications opened up by the shipping and commerce begun by the Cycladic people, the people of Crete were spurred into creativity. By 1700 B.C. they had assimilated all that their neighbors could teach them, and their own advances were so dominating that Cycladic culture was engulfed. Important to remember, though, is the cultural strain and neolithic inheritance from mainland Greece, via the Cyclades, that entered into the ultimate achievement of Crete as a civilization. We may fairly suppose that part of that inheritance was storytelling as it had developed in the region. In time, the stories would return to the mainland, enriched by Near Eastern traditions by way of Crete.

Like the Neanderthals, the people of Crete were pacific people, whom the archeologist Arthur Evans dubbed Minoans, after the legendary king, Minos. No one knows what they called themselves. They were great builders, erecting a number of grand palaces on the island from 2000 B.C. and following, the principal palace being at Knossos. These were jumbled affairs of tiny rooms as well as larger ones, terraces, light wells, stairways and passages. The palaces not only provided luxurious living quarters complete with plumbing, but included the major storerooms for the island's produce of grain, olive oil, and wine. The palaces also served as cultic centers, incorporating niches for ceremonial objects and lustral chambers for ritual bathing. Beyond the structual maze, several characteristics strike the visitor. One is the conspicuous lack of fortifications. The unwalled palaces lie open to the surroundings, and nowhere on the island are there garrisons or other indications of defense installations. Current supposition is that, as the Minoans enveloped the culture of the Cyclades, they also erradicated piracy in order to protect their growing fleet of ships that conducted trade throughout the eastern Meditarrancan. If there was a defense system, it lay at sea.

One peculiar structural device of the Minoans was the design of columns. Rising from the pavement, they flare outward and are capped by a bulbous form and a flat square stone where they meet the timbers they support, and of course, they were brightly painted. Lastly, the visitor is surrounded by walls alive with buoyant frescoes of plant forms, birds, and animals, porpoises, elegant ladies and proud youths. Everywhere

there is exuberant joy in creation, and except for the Minoan double-axe whose meaning we do not know, there is little sign of violence or warfare. Minoan culture in this was the antithesis of the Near East with its tiresome repetition in art of bloodthirsty conquerors, slaughtered enemies, and abject tribute bringers.

There is one exception to non-violence in Minoan art and that is the bull. Evidence of a bull cult in the form of "horns of consecration" stands in a court of the Knossos palace. Inside the palace, an important fresco depicts a bull dance. In the dance, youths and girls are tossed by the horns of a bull over its back, the dancers executing a sommersault, and alighting behind the bull with the help of an assistant. Obviously this is a dangerous activity. Many of the dancers must have been killed. And what of the bull after the dance? We wonder, Where did the ritual come from? What is its meaning?

In his book, *Pueblo,* Yale Professor of Art History, Vincent Scully, hypothesizes that the source is in the mythology of Cro-Magnon who painted the bull in his cave art and spread a myth of the bull into every continent. So the dance appears in ancient Crete and surfaces in the buffalo dance of American Indians. We might add the "Bull of Heaven" in the Gilgamesh tradition of the Near East as another

manifestation. A counter argument to Vincent Scully's thesis would be to observe that anyone anywhere is going to experience awe in the close presence of a bull and that a diffusionist theory of myth is unnecessary to explain a universal experience of reverence before such embodied power. It seems to me that diffusionists, such as Vincent Scully, would have a reply if there were an example of a universally known myth that was based on an experience that was not universal. For example, the flood myth. A common mythological theme is that there was a time unlike our own before a great flood. This catastrophic event brought to an end a former era and ushered in the days we live. Now, if there is a culture that could never have experienced radical flooding but has a version of the flood myth, then the spontaneous or indigenous theorists have lost the argument. And there was such a culture — the Greeks. They possessed their own version of the flood myth (Deukalion is the Greek Noah) although the mountainous region of Greece rules out all possibility of general flooding there. The notion of a catastrophic flood could not have come out of their experience but from the diffusion of myth, possibly by way of the land of two rivers.

Among the Minoans there was another possible influence from Mesopotamia, or perhaps from the Egyptians, we are not sure, but the Minoans, about 2000 B.C. acquired knowledge of writing and began their own system of pictographs which developed into a script known today as Linear A. Only a few hundred tablets of Linear A have survived and the writing has never been deciphered. Scholarly judgment is that the tablets we do possess are merely accounting records and inventories. So the Minoans left no literature that would give direct information about their storytelling or even about their history. We would like very much to know about two principal events in their history which we know only by archeological evidence. Just as Crete was becoming the major cultural center of the Aegean, all the palaces on the island suffered destruction at one time. The supposition is that there was a great earthquake, not an invasion, for the palaces were immediately rebuilt and the culture continued to develop without interruption. Also there

was no defense construction against further attack. Nevertheless, we would like to know more about this period.

The second major event is too complicated to summarize here with any of its ambiguities, but about 1450 B.C., with the exception of Knossos, all the palaces were destroyed again, this time by fire, and a new culture arose. Although Minoans continued to live on Crete, palace life at Knossos ceased as it was known. Instead of the pacific culture of the Minoans there arose the warrior-like culture of Mycenaean Greeks who had begun settling among the Minoans.

For several hundred years there had been trade with Mycenae, on the mainland of Greece, and seemingly a colony of Mycenaeans lived on Crete. During that period of amity, Linear A, which we assume was used to transcribe the Minoan tongue, was adapted to transcribe the Proto-Greek of the Mycenaeans. This second form of Minoan script is called Linear B. It was in use on Crete well before 1450 B.C. and continued to be used afterward. It was adopted by the Mycenaeans on the mainland and thousands of Linear B tablets have been found in both places.

Linear B is the kind of link historians like to have in tracing cultural influences. In this case, it is clear that Minoan civilization had impact on Greece as verified by other kinds of archeological evidence, such as pottery and Minoan-style pillars. Not the least in inheritance might be the storytelling of the Minoans, although the Minoans left us not a clue in their own land. From the Greeks, however, we gain a number of stories about the people of Crete, whether they are Greek in origin or whether the stories are essentially Minoan. And what great stories they are. To this day they supply us with words, names, and story events we use as common parlance.

Basically, there are two cycles of stories, each centered on an individual, and not surprisingly involving bulls. One cycle is about the clever inventor, Daidalos. King Minos had a magnificent white bull which he promised to sacrifice to a god, but he became reluctant to lose the beast and failed to make the offering. This angered the god who, in

Lion Gate of Mycenae

reprisal, caused the wife of King Minos, Pasiphae, to fall in love with the bull and have carnal desires for it. Daidalos at the time was in the service of King Minos, and Pasiphae persuaded him to construct a mechanical cow, into which she could climb and gratify her lust for the white bull. The issue was the Minotaur ("Minos' bull"), half man and half bull. King Minos then commanded Daidalos to construct an enclosure for the Minotaur that would hide it from public view and from which it could never escape. The result of Daidalos' inventiveness was the Labyrinth. Then Daidalos fell out of favor with King Minos, and he and his son were themselves put into the Labyrinth. Their only means of escape was to fly away from Crete, so Daidalos and his son, Ikaros, constructed wings by attaching feathers to a framework with wax. Together they flew from the Labyrinth and across the Aegean. But Ikaros so delighted in the power of flight he flew too near the sun. The wax that held the feathers melted and he plummeted into the sea below.

This cycle of stories echoes the religious significance of the bull to the Minoans and suggests that following the bull dance, the animal was sacrificed to a god. Because of the high estimation of the bull, the sacrifice would be the most perfect offering at an altar. Perhaps the impressive double-axe, so prominent in Minoan decoration, was the instrument of sacrifice. As for the Labyrinth, not a trace of it has been found on Crete. Probably it is simply a reflection of the palace at Knossos. To the Mycenaneans, the size of the palace and the jumbled arrangement of the several floors of rooms and passageways would create the impression of a maze where one could easily become lost.

A dim recollection of Cretan sources of many Greek myths may be expressed in the tradition that the great god Zeus was born and raised on Crete. And there is a sure echo in the myth of Zeus transforming himself into a white bull to attract Europa and make off with her to Crete.

The other cycle of stories revolves around Theseus, prince of Athens. King Minos' son was shamelessly murdered by the Athenians after he

Double-axe pattern on Cretan pottery

had won a prize at the Panathenian games. In reprisal, King Minos demanded the tribute every nine years of seven virgins and seven youths to feed the Minotaur who ate only human flesh. On the third occasion of tribute, Theseus joined the tribute being shipped to Crete. Once inside the Labyrinth, he slew the Minotaur, and with the help of a ball of thread given him by Ariadne, King Minos' daughter, he led the Athenians out of the Labyrinth and safely home.

Again, there is the theme of the Minotaur in association with Crete and a recollection of the palace at Knossos. Equally important is the reflection of the period when the Greeks were subservient to the Minoans and King Minos could demand tribute.

The Mycenaean Greeks dominated the Aegean until 1100 B.C. During that time they grew enormously wealthy, as witness the gold burial offerings that have survived and the excavated palace of Nestor at Pylos, sumptuous beyond anything conceived by the Minoans. And then for unknown reasons, the Mycenaeans slipped into a dark age of four hundred years. Linear B, in which Proto-Greek was written, was forgotten. Ancient Greek stories and Greek history were preserved only by oral tradition until the time of Homer.

Leonard Cottrell, *The Bull of Minos.* Holt, Rinehart and Winston, N.Y., 1958
Maitland A. Edey, *Lost World of the Aegean.* Time-Life Books, N.Y., 1975
Mary Renault, *The King Must Die,* a novel. Pantheon Books, N.Y., 1958

Vincent Scully, *Pueblo.* Viking Press, N.Y., 1975
Emily Vermeule, *Greece in the Bronze Age.* University of Chicago Press, Chicago, 1972

Traditional bust of Homer

IV

IONIA

During the Dark Age of Greece, two major migrations took place. From the north, the Dorians, a Greek-speaking people, invaded Mycenae and Mycenaean Crete. The amalgamation of peoples had a happy result, and in later years they referred to the invasion as the Return of the Heraklidae (Sons of Herakles), claiming thereby their descent from the great hero.

The second migration was a general movement from all mainland Greece across the Aegean to the eastern coastline of the Sea. This migration included the people of Mycenae, Attica, and the regions farther north. The movement was a natural result of population growth and did not have the character of colonization, as typical in later centuries. Then, when city states swelled with people, they financed outposts for emigrants who would be faithful to the mother city, perpetuate her cults and civilization, and also bring in the advantages of colonial expansion. Because this movement of population we now speak of was not colonization but a true migration, in the settlements across the Aegean there was a mixture of Greek peoples free to evolve

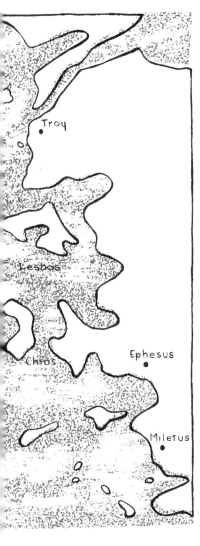

their own unique culture as they found themselves together in a strange place. For the sake of simplicity we will speak of this culture as Ionian, although strictly speaking the northern settlements were known as Aeolian and the southern as Carian.

We need to gain an understanding of Ionian culture for reasons that will soon be apparent. Perhaps the terrain affected the development of these eastern Greeks, but whatever it was, they did create a principal characteristic of Greek civilization as we think of it. The coastline of the eastern Aegean was a narrow shelf at best. Rugged, sharply folded mountains came down to the sea and the ridges frequently appeared again off-shore as tiny islands. The coastline itself was extremely jagged and there was little visual stretch up or down, each small community cut off and isolated. With the mountains to their back, the Ionians looked out across the sea to mainland Greece, and if there was a focus it was on Athens. There was no sense of their new homeland being Asiatic or that they would become Asiatics.

At first, the Ionians felt like "outlanders" and they made little attempt at pretense. Their virtue was not to be seen in physical things but in individual character. Consequently, their architecture was merely serviceable, their pottery practical and dull. Where they excelled was in the mind, and in that they were incomparable. A glimpse ahead in time will reveal the fruits of the genius already developing. In this glimpse we will keep an eye on the coastline and let chronology fall by the way.

Beginning in the south, there is Miletus which in time grew to be a powerful maritime center. It was also the home of Thales, the first thoroughgoing rationalist who refused to accept any assumption that did not prove to him reasonable, and so he is thought of as the first philosopher. In his scientific work, he began with data and attempted to give explanations of them, while he also sought a unifying theory of matter. His pupil, Anaximander, became an even finer scientist, and it was he who first postulated on the basis of marine fossils found on a mountain top, that living beings began in the sea and man evolved from the fish.

Ephesus produced Herodotus, whom Cicero called the father of history. There had been mythographers before Herodotus, but it was he who sifted evidence for historic fact, visiting battle sites in person, and searching, especially, for the reasons of the Persian Wars. To the north was Lesbos. There Sappho joined in an academy for young women and was instrumental, along with Alcaeus, in developing the Lesbian tradition of lyric poetry. Plato called her "the tenth Muse." A paean to Ionian achievement could go on and on. They were remarkable people, and in this rapid view ahead we already gain a sense of Ionic character, of its essential stress on the mind.

The close of the Dark Age throughout Greece came with the introduction of the Phoenician alphabet which was adapted to the sound of Greek language and expanded to include vowels. In their written language, the Phoenicians like the Hebrews managed without vowel signs, but the rich sounds of Greek speech would leave too many ambiguities if their written language did not include vowels. With a means of writing, far simpler than the complex system of Linear B, and a growing literacy, Greek culture made great advances in the eighth century. During the Dark Age oral tradition preserved memories of the past, the folk lore, and the myths that give a people a sense of who they are and to whom they belong. Not surpisingly, the center of this oral tradition, dependent on the mind's memory, was in Ionia, principally on the island of Chios.* There, men and women trained to be aoidoi singers of tales, and learned their craft. During the Dark Age and for a time after, the aoidoi were the only professional craftsmen of any kind in Ionia and were greatly respected. The school of Chios continued for centuries, producing, for instance, Simonides, the great singer of the sixth century.

The training of an aoidos embraced three elements. Most important, of course, was to have the stories right, even if there were details that no longer made sense. If tradition had it that Philoctetes' festered foot was

*There were other important Ionian centers, such as Smyrna, but for our purpose we will focus on Chios alone.

Detail from "The Great Bronze Blade" found in the citadel at Mycenae

caused by a snake bite, it could not be by a poisonous thorn. Or if Aias' shield was like a wall, then Aias carried a shield like a wall, even if no one ever heard of such a thing and knew only of small, round ones. (Archeologists know today that the curved, vertical shield of the Mycenaeans was like a full-length, protective wall and oral tradition accurately preserved this information.) This conservatism, even archaism, antithetical to some storytelling today that insists on modernization of our venerable heritage of stories, was of the essence of storytelling. And because of his link with the past, the storyteller was held in universal respect.

Second, an aoidos learned the techniques of casting stories in sung hexameters. Long formulary events that naturally repeat themselves with frequency in stories, such as putting on armor, would be memorized entirely and altered as need be when reciting a particular story. Shorter epithets used to modify a person or god were a handy way to fill out a line of hexameter verse, and hundreds of epithets of varying

By the Achilles Painter, c. 440 B.C.

length and accent were memorized for every possible need. Skills were also developed to memorize entire passages, especially if the passages involved messages or dreams, because they would have to be repeated without variance. A message or dream would be told first when it was given or experienced, and again when it was received or interpreted. Even a casual listener to the tale would discern any discrepency between the two tellings and fault the teller for poor craftsmanship.

Third, an aoidos learned to play the kithara as shown here. These instruments of eight to eleven strings had a wood sounding board of sufficient resonance for the strings to be heard by a large audience, and it was the musical instrument of professional singers. Amateurs accompanied themselves on the lyre with a sounding board made of leather stretched over a tortoise shell. The lyre produced only feeble resonance and stopping of the strings after each note was less critical. It was typical of Alexander the Great that when he was a youth he learned to play the kithara while his idol in the *Iliad*, Achilleus, merely played the lyre (*Iliad* IX, 186).

Quickly, as one studies this picture of an aoidos and reflects on the Standard of Ur, differences become apparent. In the earlier situation, the singer and player needed to have a firmer, fixed text known to both while the aoidos, accompanying himself, could be freer and more inventive during a performance. However, in the abstract we could come to conclusions that would evaporate in the presence today of two gifted jazz musicians singing and playing a "standard." Whatever the differences behind the two traditions, there were skill and an understanding of how to go about producing a successful result that measured up to their art.

Of course, there was much more for the aoidos to learn — how to present himself with style, how to control an audience, how to deal with rudeness, how to gain a greater purse for his work. At the school of Chios he learned from masters and practiced with his equals.

During the critical period of transition from the Dark Age to the literate Classic Age, one aoidos rose above all others. In fact, Homer remains the greatest storyteller of all time. A number of conflicting traditions attached themselves to him so that today little can be said about him with certainty. His time can be reckoned as late eighth and early seventh centuries, and possibly he was born in Smyrna. The oldest tradition is that he belonged to the school of aoidoi on Chios. Supposedly he was blind and most probably he was illiterate. His gifts to the world were two momumental epics, the *Iliad* and the *Odyssey*. Both works concern the heroic age when the Mycenaeans brought about the fall of Troy and then returned home.

Thanks to Homer, we gain in the *Odyssey* (VIII, 28f) a valuable picture of storytelling as remembered from the time before the Dark Age. Odysseus' raft has broken up and he swims to the shore of the Phaiakians where he is received by the king, Alkinnoös, who declares to his people:

'Here is this stranger, I do not know who he is, come wandering
suppliant here to my house from the eastern or western people.
He urges conveyance, and entreats us for its assurance.
So let us, as we have done before, hasten to convey him,
for neither has any other man who has come to my house
stayed here grieving a long time for the matter of convoy.
Come then, let us drag a black ship down to the bright sea,
one sailing now for the first time, and have for it a selection
from the district, fifty-two young men, who have been the finest
before. Then, each man fastening his oar to the oarlock,
disembark, then come to my house and make yourselves busy
for a present feast, and I will make generous provision
for all. I say this to the young men, but also, you other
sceptered kings, come to me in my splendid dwelling,
so we can entertain the stranger guest in our palace.
Let none refuse; and summon also the inspired singer
Demodokos, for to him the god gave song surpassing
in power to please, whenever the spirit moves him to singing.'
So he spoke, and led the way, and the others followed,
as sceptered kings, but a herald went seeking the inspired singer,
and also the fifty-two young men who had been selected
went, as he told them, along the beach of the barren salt sea.

But when they had come down to the sea, and where the ship was,
they dragged the black ship down to the deeper part of the water,
and in the black hull set the mast in place, and set sails,
and made the oars fast in the leather slings of the oarlocks
all in good order, and hoisted the white sails and set them.
They anchored her deep enough in the channel, and then themselves
made their way to the great house of wise Alkinoös,
and the porticoes and enclosures and rooms were filled with people
assembling, there were many men there, both old and young ones,
and for them Alkinoös made a sacrifice, twelve sheep, eight
pigs with shining tusks, and two drag-footed oxen.
These they skinned and prepared and made the lovely feast ready.
      The herald came near, bringing with him the excellent singer
whom the Muse had loved greatly, and gave him both good and evil.
She reft him of his eyes, but she gave him the sweet singing
art. Pontonoös set a silver-studded chair out for him
in the middle of the feasters, propping it against a tall column,
and the herald hung the clear lyre on a peg placed over
his head, and showed him how to reach up with his hands and take it
down, and set beside him a table and a fine basket,
and beside him a cup to drink whenever his spirit desired it.
They put forth their hands to the good things that lay ready before them.
But when they had put away their desire for eating and drinking,
the Muse stirred the singer to sing the famous actions
of men on that venture, whose fame goes up into the wide heaven,
the quarrel between Odysseus and Peleus' son, Achilleus . . . .
Then Alkinoös spoke:
      'Hear me, you leaders of the Phaiakians and men of counsel.
By this time we have filled our desire for the equal feasting
and for the lyre, which is the companion to the generous
feast. Now let us go outside and make our endeavor
in all contests, so that our stranger can tell his friends, after
he reaches his home, by how much we surpass all others
in boxing, wrestling, leaping and speed of our feet for running.'
      So he spoke, and led the way, and the rest went with him,
and the herald hung up the clear lyre on its peg, and taking
Demodokos by the hand he led him out of the palace . . .*

*Translated by Richmond Lattimore. Reprinted by permission of Harper &
  Row, Publishers, Inc.

45

The genius of Homer lay, not only in his grip on the techniques of his craft, but in his ability to subsume vast amounts of legendary/mythological material within a small, human-scale framework. Thus, the events that propelled the Mycenaeans to attack Troy and hold the ten-year siege of the city are contracted into a few weeks just before the fall, leaving the final debacle to everyone's knowledge of the outcome. Even more, Homer so humanized the military expedition that it becomes merely the background for his real story, the wrath of Achilleus. As his hearers would expect, Homer goes into lurid details of slaughter on the battlefield, but the overall feeling is Homer's sense of foolishness and waste of warfare. He uses this monstrous evil to bring into as sharp a light as possible the heroic virtues of persons and the pathos of human tragedies. It is this warm, genuine humanism that characterizes all Homer's work. And because this quality marks the *Odyssey* equally as the *Iliad*, we can still assume they are the creation of the same aoidos even though there are scholarly reasons to suspect the hands of others in the epics as we have received them.

A crucial question for our purpose is, What compelled Homer to compose his epics? Both are of enormous length. It is inconceivable that a single aoidos could recite either one in less than a couple of weeks. At the crudest level of argument, the human voice can stand only so much strain before it demands a rest. Further, a teller needs time following the recitation of one episode to gain a clear overview of the structure of the next episode before he can risk the telling of it. Now, in Homer's day there was absolutely no occasion for such a tour de force. Socrates might go from one soiree to another the next night without sleep, but they were separate soirees. Banquets, which were the principal occasions for hiring aoidoi, lasted only one night. Conceivably, a host might entertain a special guest with a series of banquets for a week, but not for several weeks. Religious observances never lengthened out to such an extreme, either. And there was no religious occasion, besides, that the subject matter of either epic suited.*

*The same questions surround music's equivalent to the Homeric epics, the

If we recall Homer's period in history, however, we see the occasion clearly. The occasion was the recovery of literacy. For centuries the stories that Homer drew on to create his epics had been sustained by oral tradition and held in the memories of the aoidoi. But with the ancient stories being written down, life was going out of them. (Plato's *Phaedrus* is a philosophic treatment of the problem.) Memory had been the chief gift and instrument of the aoidos. Not the short-term memory of retaining stories from a written document to be recited the next day, but a memory that spanned generations and held the inheritance as a sacred trust, for otherwise it would be lost. Memory personified, in Greek thought, was the mother of the Muses, and it was the Muses that spoke through Homer. As he said,

> Tell me now, you Muses who have your homes in Olympos.
> For you, who are goddesses, are there, and you know all things,
> and we have heard only the rumor of it and know nothing.*

Once the storyteller's lore was written down and sealed forever in the letters of the written word, the Muses became dispensable. The strong feeling was that the Muses departed when the words were written and with them the authority that verified and testified to the myths and folk tales as recited by the inspired aoidos. For Homer, it was the last chance to gather the oral tradition together into two great cycles of storytelling. The challenge to this supreme artist was to create the simple, all-embracing framework for his epics and to cast the traditional material in the most perfect mosaic of formulae, epithets, and every other device of storytelling possible. Illiterate Homer summed up for posterity the period of storytelling that was coming to a close.

The likelihood is that he did not, as often assumed, dictate his epics to scribes. Rather, the school of aoidoi on Chios gathered for those ex-

---

Bach B minor Mass. This score, never performed in Bach's lifetime and totally impractical for liturgy, and unsuitable for any other purpose, is simply the greatest work of man in music. Why did Bach write it? Perhaps for many of the same reasons Homer composed the *Iliad*. Greatness will out.

Iliad II, 485 Translated by Richmond Lattimore

traordinary weeks when Homer first performed the lengthy, revolutionary recitals. It must have been like Woodstock and Madame Schumann-Heink's farewell all put together. The gathered aoidoi, practiced in the skills of memorization, let their minds be imprinted by the performances, and from then on the effort of bringing recall would be to remember Homer's tellings. So an age ended forever and a new one was coming into being. These new aoidoi became known as the Homeridai, Sons of Homer. During the next hundred or so years, individual Homeridai made private notes of how the epics should be sung, and slowly these personal notes became public and began to circulate among other storytellers than the school of Chios, and the Homeridai faded away.

Returning to the overall view of this essay, it is a curious coincidence that as the Greek heritage of stories was taking on a definitive form in Homer's epics and written down by various Homeridai the oral tradition of the Hebrews was also becoming fixed in traditions scholars designate as J, E, D, and P. And just as stunning is the fact that both the Greek and Hebrew works carried along the tradition of even greater age, the storytelling of Sumer. The Hebrew Pentateuch not only records the Hebrew's understanding of the Sumerian flood myth, but much of the Old Testament is shot through with references to Sumerian mythology. The Pentateuch as we have it now is largely prose, but like the Homeric epics, its origins were in the storyteller's easiest style, that is, sung verse. We are fortunate to have an example of the transition in the *Book of Judges.* The final editor of *Judges* appended a footnote to chapter four, adding chapter five which was the original source of chapter four as it was once sung. This Song of Deborah was obviulsy

Proto-Ionic capital

Ionic capital

a women's piece and is further evidence that there were women singers of tales among the Hebrews as among the Greeks, and as among the Sumerians.

Homer, too, shows the abiding influence of Sumer. The story of the relationship between Achilleus and Patroklos bears remarkable similarity to the story of Gilgamesh and Enkidu, and importantly both epics have their structural turning point at the death of the companions. The *Odyssey*, with all its fantastic tales and extraordinary personages, clearly reflects the fantastic elements of the Gilgamesh epic. These tales still move us today and excite our imaginations, probably because they are almost as old as mankind itself.

There is one intriguing visual confirmation of Sumerian influence in Ionia that parallels Homer's echoes of the *Epic of Gilgamesh.* As we have seen, the Ionians did not excel in the plastic, visual arts. But there is one exception, and that is the Ionic capital. Compared with the Doric capitol of mainland Greece, it exhibits unexpected elegance and grace. This form of great beauty, as we study it, clearly derives from the oft-repeated graphic symbol of the tree of life in Mesopotamia, just as that tree of life becomes a literary symbol and finds a place in the Hebrew's garden of Eden in *Genesis.*

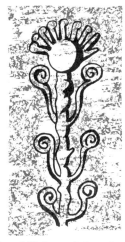

Tree of life from cylinder seal, 9th or 8th century

Richmond Lattimore, *The Iliad of Homer.* University of Chicago Press, Chicago, 1951

Richmond Lattimore, *Odyssey of Homer*. Harper & Row, New York, 1968

J. M. Cook, *The Greeks in Ionia and the East*. Frederick A. Praeger, N.Y., 1962

Rhys Carpenter, *Folk Tales, Fiction and Saga in the Homeric Epics*. University of California Press, Berkeley, 1956

John Forsdyke, *Greece Before Homer: Ancient Chronology and Mythology*. W. W. Norton & Company Inc., N.Y., 1964

G. S. Kirk, *The Songs of Homer*. Cambridge University Press, N.Y., 1962

V

ATHENS

For the next two hundred years the Homeridai perpetuated the Homeric tradition, singing the *Iliad* and *Odyssey* to the kithara as Homer had done. They travelled throughout Ionia and crossed the Aegean to mainland Greece, spreading their knowledge and love of this unique heritage that belonged to all Greeks. As faithfully as possible they repeated the epics as they had received them. Possibly during this period, however, one or two extraordinary singers added an extended ending to the *Iliad* and inserted Book X, and these, too, became part of the tradition. Also, in counterpoint to Homer, another voice became known shortly after. Hesiod, a discontent younger brother, left with the smaller part of the brothers' inheritance, and farming the land for what it brought, wrote two works that became honored second only to Homer's. They strike me like Ben Franklin's *Poor Richard's Almnac*, but he does give the earliest written clues to some myths and tales that loomed later in art, poetry, and drama.

Other aoidoi created entirely new works in the spirit and technique of Homer, making use of common material that had not suited Homer's

Detail from crater, c. 750 B.C.

purposes. These new works, known collectively as the Epic Cycle, satisfied natural curiosity and the desire to know more about the events and heroes of Homer's stories. The phenomenon is paralleled today by sequels to box office hit films, and like our sequels the poems of the Epic Cycle were a bit thin, but no harm done.

Then about the beginning of the sixth century, the styles of the Homeridai and aoidoi had run their courses. Literacy and a growing sophistication made demands for new forms and new styles to suite the day. Probably the old ways seemed too archaic, too much like the geometric pottery of the past. Geometric style was too predictable, too restricted for the new taste. What was called for was greater liveliness and the daring of individual spontaneity. The new spirit was reflected also in storytelling.

On Lesbos, Sappho and Alcaeus continued writing lyric poetry, short works, in contrast to the lengthy epics, reflecting their personal experiences of life rather than retelling the corporate lore. The new genre suited the times and had enormous effect that was felt throughout Greece.

At the same time, the Homeridai were replaced by rhapsodes. Like the Homeridai, the rhapsodes continued to recite Homer, but in a new, freer style that spoke with immediacy to the listeners. The major innovation was that they no longer sang Homer's words, but recited them. Instead of singing with a kithara, as the aoidoi did, they stood holding a staff called a rhabdos.

From a vase by Kleitias, c. 570 B.C.

From an amphora, c. 400 B.C.

The change of presentation was revolutionary. It had effect on the teller as well as the listeners. A new day had come in the development of storytelling. The kithara had always been something of a handicap. It was held upright by a hidden cord that looped about the singer's neck, leaving both hands free as demanded to play the instrument. With one hand, the aoidos plucked the strings with a plectrum while the other hand was used to stop the virbation of each string. With both hands occupied in playing the kithara, there was little chance for a dramatic gesture. In contrast, the rhapsode, no longer tied to the awkward musical instrument, stood in a commanding posture and was free to move about, to gesture, and furthermore he had his rhabdos to use as a prop.

From vase paintings it appears that the rhabdos did not differ very much from the usual walking stick, although it was always topped by a handle and was a fine one. Probably the custom of the rhabdos stemmed from the democratic spirit that marked the Greek character. Even under a monarchical system, freemen were always able to speak up to their leader in assembly. We see such a scene in *Iliad* II, 279. A sceptre was used in assembly and the man to whom the sceptre was passed had the floor. Later, when the rhapsodes held contests, a rhabdos was used, as they stood in a circle, and the rhapsode holding it had his turn and no one could interrupt. By the same token, it was also part of the contest for the reciting rhapsode suddenly to toss the rhabdos to another rhapsode, who was expected to continue Homer's hexameters without a break. If he failed, it was a mark against him in the judges' estimation. As a symbol of the contests and his profession, each rhapsode in his travellings carried his own rhabdos and used it in his solo performances.

There were two further consequences of the rhapsode speaking the words of the epics rather than singing them. For one thing, there was less opportunity to improvise over a hiatus when memory temporarily failed. With the benefit of having a musical instrument, an aoidos could extend a passage with musical flourishes or even simple beat without losing momentum. But a rhapsode standing alone before an audience without the support of musical improvisation, needed to have a firmer grasp of the poetry. For another thing, there needed to be a more fluid style of delivery markedly different from the archaic style slowed by the singing. This more rapid pacing contributed to a dramatic effect that was reinforced by the rhapsode's mobility and gesturing. The new style was truly revolutionary.

The faster pace of the rhapsode meant a greater need for memorization, but this did not curb a growing corruption of the Homeric text. On the contrary, the new dramatic style encouraged embellishments and strivings for effects. With this increasingly personalized performance of the epics, the rhapsode became more and more a celebrity in his own right. He became foppish and opened himself to the satire of a Plato, as in the *Ion* where Socrates, with tongue in cheek, says, "I often envy the profession of a rhapsode, Ion; for you have always to wear fine clothes, and to look as beautiful as you can is part of your art." That poor Ion did not get the barb simply emphasizes how general were the rhapsode's airs. Nevertheless, the rhapsodes were very popular and always drew audiences, especially at festivals where they held contests. Under the pressure of competition they outdid themselves to gain first prize.

The festival occasions were many. Among them were the rites of Asklepios, the god of medicine, held principally in Epidauros and the games of Olympia, Delphi, Nemea, and Isthmia. But the critical occasion, for the history of storytelling, came in Athens. In the sixth century, a remarkable man, Pisistratus, became tyrant of Athens and he effected a number of reforms of lasting consequence. (The term, "tyrant," has accrued overtones that originally did not belong to it.) One reform of his had to do with a traditional Athenian holiday every four years when the women of the city, having made a new, rich peplos, or garment, replaced it for the old one on the statue of Athene in her temple on the acropolis. Everyone who belonged to greater Athens, the country folk as well as the city people, gathered within the walls, and the women would parade through the streets with the new peplos. After the ceremony at the temple there would be athletic contests and contests among the rhapsodes who came from all Greece. Athens at this time was becoming a distinguished city, spurred on by the inpetus of Solon, and Pisistratus saw that the Panathenea could be instrumental in developing further the citizens' pride in their polis. In his restructuring of the Panathenea, he laid down new rules for the contest of the rhapsodes. The only epics that could be recited in competition were the *Iliad* and the *Odyssey*, and in whole. Scholars disagree about the meaning of this rule, but I take it to mean that the jocularity associated with suddenly tossing the rhabdos was forbidden. Rather, each rhapsode was to recite a whole portion of the epics with due respect for its integrity. To this same end, Pisistratus (or his son, Hipparchus) ordered that a text be made of the epics as they were known in the old time. In other words, the later accretions of the rhapsodes were excised and personal elaborations were forbidden. The stories must be told as they always had been and within that framework the rhapsode's art was to be practiced. The supposition must be that the written notes of the Homeridai were the basis of the new authorized text and that this Athenian recension is essentially the epics as we have received them.

During this period, the storytelling heritage was being put to new use in a new way. The reform of Pisistratus had reestablished the epics' primacy over flamboyant virtuosity of individual rhapsodes, and while the epics were not sung as in the old days, their effect was traditional. But growing sophistication of the Greeks required a new expression that reflected the times, and the result was choral poetry. Lyric poetry recited by a single performer was typical of Lesbos across the Aegean. It was their way of continuing the tradition of the aoidoi while searching new, creative grounds. On the mainland, poetry began to be written for group performance to suite their temperament. The subject matter was still the myths and legends of old, but they were now given multimedia treatment. The technique culminated in the odes of Pindar of Thebes, but the style began a century earlier.

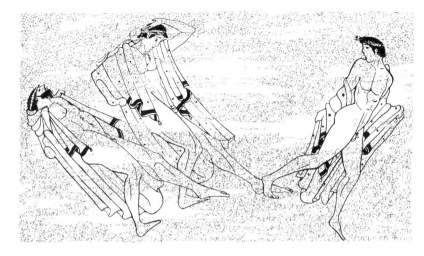

By the Brygos Painter, c. 480 B.C.

This is the general pattern of events: A young man, Aristokleideas of Aigina, wins the prize for the pankration at the Nemean games. His proud father, Aristophanes, commissions Pindar to create a choral ode to commemorate the victory. After many months, perhaps a year, Pindar travels to Aigina and there trains the youth's friends for the performance. Beautifully robed and garlanded, they will sing the ode to music Pindar has composed,* with accompaniment of flute and lyre, and executing a choreography created by Pindar for the occasion. Typically, the ode begins with an acknowledgement of the father and the youth's proud city. This reminds the poet of a myth or legend which he then relates in part, and finally he ingeniously ties the story to the youth's victory.

Clearly, the effect of choral odes must have been stunning and justified their enormous expense. Pindar did not work cheaply and his expense account could amount to a tidy sum. But storytelling, in such multimedia extravaganzas, had moved light years from the simplicity of

*We are fortunate to have a fragment of Pindar's music for an ode, for almost all classical Greek music has been lost although the Greeks felt that their music was their greatest artistic achievement. Of course, we also have many of Pindar's odes.

a travelling aoidos who accompanied himself with a kithara and shared the heritage that belonged to everyone. If his story was relevant to the occasion, his hearers could make the association themselves. *His principal obligation was to his story material even if in some ways it was no longer comprehensible.* The new style of choral poetry fitted the times, like Art Deco in the twenties or Happenings in the sixties. It made the stories relevant, and by combining a number of art forms, created a spectacle that was memorable.

During the time of this evolution leading to Pindar, there was a second development leading to Aeschylus and the birth of tragic drama. We can imagine in the unfettered days of rhapsodes, when they no longer sang Homer but recited him and felt free to improvise, their performances took on histrionics. That is, as the story unfolded the rhapsode differentiated the voices of the characters in a scene, as any good storyteller would do. It was a simple but giant step to move from this quasi-impersonation to full impersonation of a character. Then the storyteller ceased to be storyteller and became actor. This was the achievement of Thespis. Thespis created a new form of presentation in which he impersonated the major character of a story and played out his role, from start to finish, with the assistance of a chorus which responded to the character and his situation as the audience might. It is important to see that this development came from the tradition of the storyteller and not, as long assumed, from the dithyramb or other forms of choral poetry. In the works of Thespis, he played the character from a traditional tale and he wrote the lines for the chorus who acted as a baffle to the hero's unfolding plight. And always the story material had to do with some fatality that would deeply move the audience.

In the creativity of Thespis we see the beginning of drama, and one wonders why it was so long a time in coming. That drama did evolve from the tradition of the storyteller can be seen in the curious word first used to name drama, tragedy. Tragedy literally means ''goat song'' in Greek, which of itself makes little sense. But if we know that at the con-

Actor with mask and elevated on cothurus boots

tests of rhapsodes the prize was often a goat, then we can understand why a rhapsode was a "goat singer" since he frequently sang for a goat. And when we remember that Thespis extrapolated the rhapsodes' impersonations during storytelling and created a single impersonation for an actor, the new art form could properly though awkwardly be called a "goat song," that is, a work that might be performed by a "goat singer."

About all that could be done with storytelling had been done by the first century B.C. Although there had been mythographers, it remained for Ovid and later, Apuleius, to take the final step. That was, to separate themselves from live performance and write coherent novels for readership. The *Metamorphoses* of Ovid and *The Golden Ass* of Apuleius are wonderful in their way, but they bring to a close a long, long chapter of communal, oral storytelling. The artist now directed himself to a sheet of paper in his solitude and what he wrote would be read by someone distant and temporally separated from him, even by us today. What no one wrote, however, was an epitaph for live storytelling. Storytelling would continue as long as man had a memory or a dream, and as long as he congregated at a pit fire as a social being.

Gerald F. Else, *The Origin and Early Form of Greek Tragedy*. W. W. Norton & Company, Inc., N.Y. 1965

Richmond Lattimore, *The Odes of Pindar*. University of Chicago Press, Chicago. Second edition, 1976

Mary Renault, *The Praise Singer*, a novel. Pantheon Books, N.Y., 1978

Musique de la Grece Antique (Music of Ancient Greece), Harmonia Mundi, France, HM 1015 (12″ lp sponsored by UNESCO)

C. M. Bowra, *Heroic Poetry*. St. Martin's Press, N.Y., 1952. (See especially chapter 15 for history of the bard to the present day.)

Hellenistic bronze horse from Chios, removed to Venice

VI

SOME REFLECTIONS

Somewhere in this survey of early traditions of storytelling the reader recognizes the beginnings of his style of telling, its functions, and its limitations. All subsequent styles are variants of these original, basic modes, and within them lie our roots.

The naive teller at the pit fire who has not made a conscious effort at self-training but simply does what comes naturally, perhaps unconsciously following the model of another storyteller, and improving by repetition and experience, is the backbone of storytelling. This tradition is the continuing undergirding of all storytelling. It is the fundamental constant and the source of all further development. Even the epics of Homer are erected of building materials that originally came from the naive teller. There are scores of marchën (fairy tales) and other folk tales that lie behind the *Iliad* and *Odyssey*, and essentially it is only Homer's professional grasp of the material and his grand-scale vision that separate him from the naive teller at the pit fire or a parent at a child's bedside.

The naive teller is at his best when he is most artless, when he is not striving for effect, but telling from a long memory the stories he has known since childhood, or events in his life that have helped shape him and make him who he is.

To say "artless' does not mean to be dull and lifeless. It means avoidance of artifice, or being cute or precious. There is a natural gift of storytelling that we must have inherited, it comes so unpremeditatedly and easily if only we get our inhibitions out of the way and give ourselves to the act of storytelling. Our hearers supply us with the clues how best to tell, and our inner sense of the story, coming alive in our mind's eye, lets us know if we are succeeding. Once a storyteller has repeatedly experienced the magic of the process, then he can begin looking for new stories that suit him, and he is on his way to building repertoire. But when building repertoire becomes a conscious process, the chances are that naivete is lost and the teller is changing styles. Without awareness of where he is headed, many dangers lie ahead.

A common fallacy among storytellers today is the belief they are continuing "the oral tradition" or even reviving it. The fact is, there is no possible way for the literate storyteller to do anything of the sort. Literacy, with the sophistication that accompanies it, brings into play wholly alien crtieria that affect one's telling. If a literate person comes upon an occasion of storytelling among illiterate people whose only tradition is oral, his perception of the event, in the first place, is skewed by his point of view and his assumptions. It is impossible for him to take part in the event as an illiterate and so be inside the occasion. He is doomed to be only a witness, and his presence as an outsider, furthermore, will have an effect on the event. What he does take note of will be screened by his values of what is noteworthy, and only the rigorous discipline of the scientific folklorist can begin to assist him. If the encounter is going to add to the storyteller's repertoire, the storyteller will need to be selective in paring down the raw experience for manageable communication, and again his values are crucial. Then with his future hearers in mind, who will be literate, he begins to reshape the selected material so that it is suitable and will bring a desired response in their lives. And when the occasion for retelling comes, the context of the telling will be entirely different from the context of the original telling, the story serving a different purpose in the lives of the hearers and having a different meaning.

It is important for us as hearers of literate, home-spun tellers of rural tales that we recognize this inescapable process and that we discern the sophisticated artistry and professionalism of these tellers. And, I feel, such tellers need even more to be self-aware and acknowledge the role of their literate culture of which they are a part in shaping their retellings. Not to do so is to be guilty of forgery, of making instant antiques for a gullible market. The legitimate thing to do is to label the performance a reproduction and not pass it off as the real thing. It would be immensely helpful if this kind of storyteller would explain the circumstance of gathering the tale, whether by himself or a scientific collector, and admit, "the tale goes *something* like this."

Faced with this problem, I believe it is a grave mistake with few exceptions for a teller to attempt a "translation' into the slang of the day or cultural equivalents, claiming that the storytelling is "in the spirit" of the original. Such a telling may shed light on our culture and make us laugh at ourselves, but seldom does such a performance reveal the truth and beauty of a culture separated from us that could enrich and broaden our lives. Such tellings rob us of the potential that was there. The reform of Pisistratus needs continually to be invoked.

As literate persons, raised in a literate society, there is no way we can carry on the oral tradition. We never belonged to it in the first place, and we cannot reenter it, like an astronaut coming back into earth's gravitational field. As much as we might like otherwise, there are passages in life and growth that are irreversible. This is one of them. But if we tell traditional tales, there are several things we can do to give depth to our tellings. We can learn as much as possible about our stories and the meaning they have in the cultures they come from. Public libraries and librarians are immensely helpful in doing this necessary research. Travel will also add invaluable authenticity to our tellings. And then we must contemplate our stories for the meanings they have for us in our lives. In all likelihood, the reason we like a particular story is becomes it pulls together into a sensible whole experiences, feelings, dreads, hopes, and fantasies we have had, or it stretches and exercises our imagination, or replies to our need to know, or calls into play the wonderful mechanism in our unconscious that results in laughter. When we understand these things, then we have truly gotten inside our stories. And we can only tell stories, truly, from the inside out. The outside of a story is simply its words — and why there should be so much fuss about the necessity of learning the words I do not understand. The hard thing is to understand a story from the inside, and once we have that insight and sense of the story's reality, then moving from inside out we will find that the traditional way of telling is just right and cannot be any other way. And then when we are ready to tell the story, we do not tell it to the Muse. The Muse already knows the story. She it was who made it come alive for us in our contemplation of it. Rather, we tell the story to those around us to whom the Muse wants to speak through us. If this strikes you as too mystical then you have not had your first experience of being a real storyteller.

To be a faithful teller is all the more important if we tell to children. In such case it is absolutely necessary to have the story just right. The first way children hear a story is the way it goes forever after, and not some other way — even if the other way, as they later find out, is the true story. To alter a story when it may be the first time it is heard by a child is to close off forever the real story for that person. Robbery has been committed, and the storyteller ought to be apprehended.

It is a great temptation, with the beautifully illustrated children's books we have today, to build our tellings around the pictures in a book. But the pictures are only one way one person, the artist, saw the story in his mind's eye. The illustrations say only what the story means to that artist. Folk stories in themselves are never so specific and they leave the hearers to build their own images with the greatest significance for them in their own lives, as Bruno Bettelheim has demonstrated. Just how varied the artists' conceptions can be is shown in Iona and Peter Opie's book, *The Classic Fairy Tales.* If professional illustrations are shown, encourage children first to make their own illustrations and then say, "Here is how somebody else saw the story."

Combining book illustrations with storytelling is to engage in multimedia with all the impact of a multi-sensory experience. Pindar seems to have sensed the dangers in multimedia for he always left open wide vistas in his works for his audience to employ their imaginations and not be confined to Pindar's only. Pindar never fully tells a myth or legend. He relies on his audience to know the story and to have personal, private understandings of it. He merely alludes to it in a striking, novel way and connects it to present events or the city where people live.

There are a few storytellers today who wear a costume and assume the role of a character in a story or cycle of stories. We can now recognize that they are in the tradition of Thespis, and that what they are creating is one-man theatre. They have ceased being storyteller and have become actor. To point this out is not to be pejorative but to make an important distinction. In true storytelling, the storyteller, even though he differentiates the characters in a story, always remains himself. As storytellers we are not called upon to have the skill and talent to be believably someone else, as an actor is. What we are called on to be is an authentic person ready to establish personal relationships with others and to share our common heritage of stories of which the storyteller is the repository. The storyteller then becomes a symbol to others of the lore that is their roots. That is why there is such universal respect of the storyteller. Plato's Ion, on the other hand, was the butt of satire because he was not an authentic person and as a wayward rhapsode he had drifted into theatrics.

There is one assurance. Whatever we do to storytelling today as professionals, amateur storytelling will continue the tradition. It always has. What we can hope for and strive toward is so perfectly to relay the heritage, even to create something new, that our hearers' lives are made richer, more lucid, and that there has been encounter between teller and hearer, and that the social bond is made stronger, as *Homo erectus* experienced around the pit fire.

Bruno Bettelheim, *The Uses of Enchantment: The Meaning and Importance of Fairy Tales.* Alfred A. Knopf, N.Y., 1976
Iona and Peter Opie, *The Classic Fairy Tales.* Oxford University Press, London, 1974

Of this limited first edition, numbered and signed,
this is number *177*

John Harrell